PERSONAL INFORMATION

COPYRIGHT

TABLE OF CONTENTS

INTRODUCTION

Welcome to your Peace of Mind and Heart Planners.

This book is designed to make life-planning as simple, user friendly, and stress-free as possible.

Your Planner is a comprehensive, customizable, all-in-one workbook to record your vital information, personal wishes, and final messages to loved ones.

It is a valuable gift for those left behind so that they can ensure your instructions are fulfilled accordingly, and to help avoid duress or confusion by planning in advance.

We have provided plenty of space to customize each section as per your needs, and include additional overflow space at the end of the book if required. It is wise to begin with the initial personal identification section first, and then proceed to one chapter at a time, collecting all the documentation and information in advance for efficiency sake.

Remember to update this planner as changes to your circumstances arise, such as new employment, investments, insurance, or adjustments to your personal wishes.

Please remember, this planner is not considered a legal document and should not be considered a formal will.

<u>*Always store this workbook somewhere safe, to prevent sensitive, private information from getting into the wrong hands*</u>.

PERSONAL INFORMATION

Legal Name

Address

Mailbox or P.O. Box Number

Mailbox Location

Key Location

Primary Phone Numbers

Spouse's Name / Maiden Name

Children's Names

Grandchildren's Names

My Dependents Names Include

Pet Names

Notes

Siblings Names

Mother's Name / Maiden Name

Father's Name

Ex-Spouse's Name/s

Notes

AT THE TIME OF PASSING

Please Contact the Following People Immediately Upon My Passing or Incapacity

Spouse / Partner

Name

Contact Information

Notes

Healthcare Power of Attorney Agent

Name

Contact Information

Notes

Executor of Will

Name

Contact Information

Notes

Please Contact the Following People

Mentor

Place of Worship

Contact Information

Notes

Mentor 2

Church Name

Contact Information

Notes

Admin/Associate #1

Name

Contact Information

Notes

Admin/Associate #2

Name

Contact Information

Notes

Name

Contact Information

Relationship

Name

Contact Information

Relationship

Name

Contact Information

Relationship

Name

Contact Information

Relationship

Name

Contact Information

Relationship

Name

Contact Information

Relationship

Name

Contact Information

Relationship

Notes

Please Contact the Following Family, Friends, and Associates

Name

Contact Information

Relationship

Name

Contact Information

Relationship

Name

Contact Information

Relationship

Name

Contact Information

Relationship

Name

Contact Information

Relationship

Name

Contact Information

Relationship

Name

Contact Information

Relationship

Notes

Please Contact the Following Family, Friends, and Associates

Name

Contact Information

Relationship

Name

Contact Information

Relationship

Name

Contact Information

Relationship

Name

Contact Information

Relationship

Name

Contact Information

Relationship

Name

Contact Information

Relationship

Name

Contact Information

Relationship

Notes

Please Contact the Following Family, Friends, and Associates

Name

Contact Information

Relationship

Name

Contact Information

Relationship

Name

Contact Information

Relationship

Name

Contact Information

Relationship

Name

Contact Information

Relationship

Name

Contact Information

Relationship

Name

Contact Information

Relationship

Notes

Additional Key Contact Information

Accountant and Book Keeper

Name #1

Contact Information

Name #2

Contact Information

Notes

Lawyer #1

Name

Contact Information

Notes

Lawyer #2

Name

Contact Information

Notes

Estate Planner

Name

Contact Information

Notes

Financial Planner

Company and Agent Name

Contact Information

Financial Planner

Company and Agent Name

Contact Information

Stock Broker

Company and Agent Name

Contact Information

Business Employer / Associate

Company and Agent Name

Contact Information

Business Employer / Associate

Company and Agent Name

Contact Information

Business Employer / Associate

Company and Agent Name

Contact Information

Notes

Health Care Provider – Medical

Company and Agent Name

Contact Information

Health Care Provider – Dental

Company and Agent Name

Contact Information

Health Care Provider – Vision

Company and Agent Name

Contact Information

Health Care Provider – Other

Company and Agent Name

Contact Information

Veterinarian

Company and Agent Name

Contact Information

Veterinarian

Company and Agent Name

Contact Information

Notes

FUNERAL ARRANGEMENTS

Funeral Arrangements Contact Person

Location

Contact Information

Place of Worship

Primary Contact

Contact Information

Funeral Home

Address

Contact Information

Cemetery or Crematorium

Plot / Address

Contact Information

Funeral Insurance Policy

Company Name

Contact Information

Notes

Burial

Headstone Details

Cremation

Ashes to be shared with / spread at

Obituary

Please Include the Following

Funeral Arrangements - Celebration of Life Services

Please Read the Following Farewell to My Loved Ones During Service (Values, Lessons, Encouragement, Etc.)

Funeral Arrangements – Notes

PLACE OF WORSHIP

Place of Worship, Charities, Tithing, and Other Related Topics

The following include my requests and instructions regarding Place of Worship, Tithing, Charity Donations, Etc.

Place of Worship

Place of Worship

Charities

Charities

Tithing

Tithing

Legacy & Other Related Topics

Legacy & Other Related Topics

Legacy & Other Related Topics

MILITARY LEGACY DETAILS

Position Ranks and DoD ID Number (Service Number Pre 1969)

Location of Service #1

Date of Service

Details of Service/Deployment

Important Memories, Awards, Lessons, Follow Up, and Special Instructions

Location of Service #2

Date

Details of Service/Deployment

Location of Service #3

Date

Details of Service/Deployment

Important Memories, Awards, Lessons, Follow Up, and Special Instructions

Location of Service #4

Date

Details of Service/Deployment

Important Military Contacts

Name

Contact Information

Relationship

Name

Contact Information

Relationship

Name

Contact Information

Relationship

Name

Contact Information

Relationship

Name

Contact Information

Relationship

Name

Contact Information

Relationship

Name

Contact Information

Relationship

Notes

Important Military Contacts

Name

Contact Information

Relationship

Name

Contact Information

Relationship

Name

Contact Information

Relationship

Name

Contact Information

Relationship

Name

Contact Information

Relationship

Name

Contact Information

Relationship

Name

Contact Information

Relationship

Notes

Important Military Contacts

Name

Contact Information

Relationship

Name

Contact Information

Relationship

Name

Contact Information

Relationship

Name

Contact Information

Relationship

Name

Contact Information

Relationship

Name

Contact Information

Relationship

Name

Contact Information

Relationship

Notes

Important Military Contacts

Name

Contact Information

Relationship

Name

Contact Information

Relationship

Name

Contact Information

Relationship

Name

Contact Information

Relationship

Name

Contact Information

Relationship

Name

Contact Information

Relationship

Name

Contact Information

Relationship

Notes

ASSETS OVERVIEW – WHAT MY LOVED ONES CAN EXPECT

Personal Residence Address

Note: Please see will for detailed instructions and division of assets

PO Box Location and Address

Partner / Co-Owner Names

Contact Information

Legal Will Location and Instructions for Division of Assets

Keys Location and Miscellaneous Instructions

Alarm and Security Information

Utilities Warranties and Documentation Location

Upkeep Information and Document Location (Gardener, Etc.)

Notes

Real Estate Investment - Second Property Address

Type of Property (Residential / Commercial)

PO Box Location and Address

Partner / Co-Owner Names

Contact Information

Legal Documentation Location and Instructions

Keys Location and Miscellaneous Instructions

Alarm and Security Information

Utilities Warranties and Documentation Location

Upkeep Information and Document Location (Gardener, Etc.)

Notes

Vehicle List: Car, Motorcycle, Recreation Vehicle, Snowmobile, Etc.

Vehicle

Year/Make/Model

VIN – ID

Ownership Documentation Location

Lease / Load Information

Keys Location

Notes

Vehicle

Year/Make/Model

VIN – ID

Ownership Documentation Location

Lease / Load Information

Keys Location

Notes

Vehicle List:

Vehicle

Year/Make/Model

VIN – ID

Ownership Documentation Location

Lease / Load Information

Keys Location

Notes

Vehicle

Year/Make/Model

VIN – ID

Ownership Documentation Location

Lease / Load Information

Keys Location

Notes

Vehicle List:

Vehicle

Year/Make/Model

VIN – ID

Ownership Documentation Location

Lease / Load Information

Keys Location

Notes

Vehicle

Year/Make/Model

VIN – ID

Ownership Documentation Location

Lease / Load Information

Keys Location

Notes

Investments: Stocks, Mutual Funds, and Other

Type

Location

Account Number

Contact Person

Documentation Location

Notes

Type

Location

Account Number

Contact Person

Documentation Location

Notes

Type

Location

Account Number

Contact Person

Documentation Location

Notes

Investments:

Type

Location

Account Number

Contact Person

Documentation Location

Notes

Type

Location

Account Number

Contact Person

Documentation Location

Notes

Type

Location

Account Number

Contact Person

Documentation Location

Notes

Investments:

Type

Location

Account Number

Contact Person

Documentation Location

Notes

Type

Location

Account Number

Contact Person

Documentation Location

Notes

Type

Location

Account Number

Contact Person

Documentation Location

Notes

Insurance Benefits:

Policy Type

Location

Account Number

Contact Person

Documentation Location

Notes

Policy Type

Location

Account Number

Contact Person

Documentation Location

Notes

Policy Type

Location

Account Number

Contact Person

Documentation Location

Notes

Employer Benefits #1

Name

Account Number

Contact Person

Documentation Location

Notes

Employer Benefits #2

Name

Account Number

Contact Person

Documentation Location

Notes

Employer Benefits #3

Name

Account Number

Contact Person

Documentation Location

Notes

Retirement Benefits

Name

Account Number

Contact Person

Documentation Location

Notes

Retirement Benefits #2

Name

Account Number

Contact Person

Documentation Location

Notes

Social Security

Name

Account Number

Contact Person

Documentation Location

Notes

Other: Veteran's Benefits, Etc.

Name

Account Number

Contact Person

Documentation Location

Notes

Other:

Name

Account Number

Contact Person

Documentation Location

Notes

Other:

Name

Account Number

Contact Person

Documentation Location

Notes

Money Owed to Me

Name

Account Number

Contact Person

Documentation Location

Notes

Name

Account Number

Contact Person

Documentation Location

Notes

Name

Account Number

Contact Person

Documentation Location

Notes

Personal Items, Jewelry, and Heirlooms

Item

Location

Notes

Item

Location

Notes

Item

Location

Notes

Item

Location

Notes

Personal Items, Jewelry, and Heirlooms

Item

Location

Notes

Item

Location

Notes

Item

Location

Notes

Item

Location

Notes

Personal Items, Jewelry, and Heirlooms

Item

Location

Notes

Item

Location

Notes

Item

Location

Notes

Item

Location

Notes

Personal Items, Jewelry, and Heirlooms

Item

Location

Notes

Item

Location

Notes

Item

Location

Notes

Item

Location

Notes

Storage Company #1

Name

Address

Key Location or Combination Number

Storage Company #2

Name

Address

Key Location or Combination Number

Notes and Instructions

BUSINESS INFORMATION

Business Details

Business Name

Business Type

Address

Landlord Name

Contact Information

Lease Documentation Location

Partner / Co-Owner Name

Contact Information

Partner / Co-Owner Name

Contact Information

Partner / Co-Owner Name

Contact Information

Partner / Co-Owner Name

Contact Information

Keys Location

Notes

Associates, Employees, and Contractors

Name

Contact Information

Name

Contact Information

Name

Contact Information

Name

Contact Information

Name

Contact Information

Name

Contact Information

Name

Contact Information

Name

Contact Information

Notes

Name

Contact Information

Name

Contact Information

Name

Contact Information

Name

Contact Information

Name

Contact Information

Name

Contact Information

Name

Contact Information

Name

Contact Information

Notes

Bank Name

Address

Contact Information

Business Bank Account Number

Business Bank Account Number

Credit Card Number

Username / PIN

Credit Card Number

Username / PIN

Documentation Location

Notes

Bank Name

Address

Contact Information

Business Bank Account Number

Business Bank Account Number

Credit Card Number

Username / PIN

Credit Card Number

Username / PIN

Documentation Location

Notes

Business Information

Accountant Name

Contact Information

Lawyer

Contact Information

Insurance Agency / Agent

Contact Information

Notes on Income, Royalties, Key Accounts Etc.

Online Business Information

Business Website Name

Hosting Provider

Username and Password

Website Developer Name

Contact Information

Documentation Location

Online Income Stream #1

Online Income Stream #2

Partner / Co-Owner Name

Contact Information

Partner / Co-Owner Name

Contact Information

Partner / Co-Owner Name

Contact Information

Business Email Address Name

Username and Password

Business Email Address Name

Username and Password

Business Email Address Name

Username and Password

Notes

Notes: Instructions for Domain Name Renewal, Hosting, Expenses, Etc.

Social Media

Name

Username and Password

Name

Username and Password

Name

Username and Password

Name

Username and Password

Name

Username and Password

Name

Username and Password

Name

Username and Password

Name

Username and Password

Name

Username and Password

Accounts

Name

Username and Password

Name

Username and Password

Name

Username and Password

Name

Username and Password

Name

Username and Password

Name

Username and Password

Name

Username and Password

Name

Username and Password

Name

Username and Password

Name

Username and Password

Money I Owe to Others

Person / Company Name

Contact Information

Documentation Location

Notes

Person / Company Name

Contact Information

Documentation Location

Notes

Person / Company Name

Contact Information

Documentation Location

Notes

Person / Company Name

Contact Information

Documentation Location

Notes

Additional Notes

Additional Notes and Instructions

BANKING INFORMATION

Bank Name

Account Type and Number

Account Type and Number

Bank Online Web Address

Username and Password

Debit Card Number

Credit Card Number

CV and Password

Online Username and Password

Rewards

Notes

Bank Name

Account Type and Number

Account Type and Number

Bank Online Web Address

Username and Password

Debit Card Number

Credit Card Number

CV and Password

Online Username and Password

Rewards

Notes

Bank Name

Account Type and Number

Account Type and Number

Bank Online Web Address

Username and Password

Debit Card Number

Credit Card Number

CV and Password

Online Username and Password

Rewards

Notes

Safe Deposit Box

Bank Location

Box Number

Key Location

Contents

Safe Deposit Box

Bank Location

Box Number

Key Location

Contents

Other Credit: Credit Cards, Line of Credit, Department Stores, Etc.

Name

Account Number

Online Website

Username and Password

Name

Account Number

Online Website

Username and Password

Name

Account Number

Online Website

Username and Password

Name

Account Number

Online Website

Username and Password

Name

Account Number

Online Website

Username and Password

Notes

Other Credit: Credit Cards, Line of Credit, Department Stores, Etc.

Name

Account Number

Online Website

Username and Password

Name

Account Number

Online Website

Username and Password

Name

Account Number

Online Website

Username and Password

Name

Account Number

Online Website

Username and Password

Name

Account Number

Online Website

Username and Password

Notes

Other Credit: Credit Cards, Line of Credit, Department Stores, Etc.

Name

Account Number

Online Website

Username and Password

Name

Account Number

Online Website

Username and Password

Name

Account Number

Online Website

Username and Password

Name

Account Number

Online Website

Username and Password

Name

Account Number

Online Website

Username and Password

Notes

Mortgage, Line of Credit, Loans

Mortgage Details

Bank / Lender

Contact Information

Account Number

Documentation Location

Second Mortgage Details

Bank / Lender

Contact Information

Account Number

Documentation Location

Third Mortgage Details

Bank / Lender

Contact Information

Account Number

Documentation Location

Other

Bank / Lender

Contact Information

Account Number

Documentation Location

Notes

Line of Credit

Bank / Lender

Contact Information

Account Number

Documentation Location

Line of Credit

Bank / Lender

Contact Information

Account Number

Documentation Location

Other

Bank / Lender

Contact Information

Account Number

Documentation Location

Other

Bank / Lender

Contact Information

Account Number

Documentation Location

Notes

Loans: Cars, Student Loan, Etc.

Bank / Lender

Contact Information

Account Number

Documentation Location

Bank / Lender

Contact Information

Account Number

Documentation Location

Bank / Lender

Contact Information

Account Number

Documentation Location

Bank / Lender

Contact Information

Account Number

Documentation Location

Bank / Lender

Contact Information

Account Number

Documentation Location

Notes

IMPORTANT DOCUMENTATION LOCATION

Will

Notes

Health Care Power of Attorney Papers

Notes

Passport

Notes

Birth Certificate

Notes

Social Security Card

Notes

Drivers Licence

Notes

Marriage Certificate

Notes

Tax Documents

Notes

Divorce Papers

Notes

Life Insurance

Notes

Health Insurance - Medical

Notes

Health Insurance Location – Dental

Notes

Health Insurance Location - Vision

Notes

Health Insurance Location – Other

Notes

Funeral Insurance

Notes

Vehicle Insurance #1

Notes

Vehicle Insurance #2

Notes

Vehicle Insurance #3

Notes

Home Owner Insurance

Notes

Rental Home Insurance

Notes

Children's Insurance #1

Notes

Children's Insurance #2

Notes

Children's Insurance #3

Notes

Other Family / Dependents Insurance

Notes

Pet Insurance #1

Notes

Pet Insurance #2

Notes

Storage Insurance #1

Notes

Storage Insurance #2

Notes

Additional Notes

Other

Notes

Other

Notes

Other

Notes

Other

Notes

Other

Notes

Other

Notes

Important Documents Location - Notes

INSURANCE PROVIDER INFORMATION

Health Insurance – Primary Health

Company Name

Agents Name

Contact Information

HSA (Health Savings Account) Information

Health Insurance - Dental

Company Name

Agents Name

Contact Information

Notes

Health Insurance – Vision

Company Name

Agents Name

Contact Information

Notes

Health Insurance – Medical

Company Name

Agents Name

Contact Information

Notes

Additional Notes

Life Insurance #1

Company Name

Agents Name

Contact Information

Notes

Life Insurance #2

Company Name

Agents Name

Contact Information

Notes

Vehicle Insurance #1

Company Name

Agents Name

Contact Information

Notes

Vehicle Insurance #2

Company Name

Agents Name

Contact Information

Notes

Vehicle Insurance #3

Company Name

Agents Name

Notes

Home Owner Insurance

Company Name

Agents Name

Contact Information

Notes

Rental Home Insurance

Company Name

Agents Name

Contact Information

Notes

Children's Insurance #1

Company Name

Agents Name

Contact Information

Notes

Children's Insurance #2

Company Name

Agents Name

Contact Information

Notes

Children's Insurance #3

Company Name

Agents Name

Contact Information

Notes

Other Dependents Insurance

Company Name

Agents Name

Contact Information

Notes

Pet Insurance #1

Company Name

Vets Name

Contact Information

Notes

Pet Insurance #2

Company Name

Vets Name

Contact Information

Notes

Storage Insurance #1

Company Name

Agents Name

Contact Information

Notes

Storage Insurance #2

Company Name

Agents Name

Contact Information

Notes

Funeral Insurance

Company Name

Agents Name

Contact Information

Notes

Other Insurance

Company Name

Agents Name

Contact Information

Notes

Other Insurance

Company Name

Agents Name

Contact Information

Notes

Other Insurance

Company Name

Agents Name

Contact Information

Notes

Other Insurance

Company Name

Agents Name

Contact Information

Notes

MEDICAL INFORMATION

Health Care Power of Attorney

Name

Contact Information

Notes

Do Not Resuscitate Instructions Document Location

Notes

Organ Donor Instructions Document Location

Notes

Blood Type

Primary Care Physician

Name

Contact Information

Address

Notes

Medical Conditions

Medications

Allergies, Food Sensitivity, and Reactions

If Incapacitated Please Follow Below Requests (Further Details in DNR Document)

Preferred Hospital

Name

Contact Information

Address

Notes

Pharmacy

Name

Contact Information

Address

Notes

Caregiver Company / Person #1

Name

Contact Information

Address

Notes

Caregiver Company / Person #2

Name

Contact Information

Address

Notes

Medical Information - Notes

DEPENDENTS INSTRUCTIONS OF CARE

My Dependents

Name

Relationship

Contact Information

Personal Documentation Location

Health Conditions Documentation Location

Guardianship Instructions Documentation Location

Guardian Name

Contact Information

Primary Care Physician

Contact Information

Notes

My Dependents

Name

Relationship

Contact Information

Personal Documentation Location

Health Conditions Documentation Location

Guardianship Instructions Documentation Location

Guardian Name

Contact Information

Primary Care Physician

Contact Information

Notes

My Dependents

Name

Relationship

Contact Information

Personal Documentation Location

Health Conditions Documentation Location

Guardianship Instructions Documentation Location

Guardian Name

Contact Information

Primary Care Physician

Contact Information

Notes

My Dependents

Name

Relationship

Contact Information

Personal Documentation Location

Health Conditions Documentation Location

Guardianship Instructions Documentation Location

Guardian Name

Contact Information

Primary Care Physician

Contact Information

Notes

My Dependents

Name

Relationship

Contact Information

Personal Documentation Location

Health Conditions Documentation Location

Guardianship Instructions Documentation Location

Guardian Name

Contact Information

Primary Care Physician

Contact Information

Notes

My Dependents

Name

Relationship

Contact Information

Personal Documentation Location

Health Conditions Documentation Location

Guardianship Instructions Documentation Location

Guardian Name

Contact Information

Primary Care Physician

Contact Information

Notes

My Dependents – Pets

Name / Type of Pet

Name of Veterinarian

Contact Information

Address

License, Insurance, and Documentation Location

Health Conditions

Medications

Guardianship Instructions Documentation Location

Guardian Name

Contact Information

General Instructions of Care – Food, Habits, Exercise, Sleep, and Other Needs

My Dependents – Pets

Name / Type of Pet

Name of Veterinarian

Contact Information

Address

License, Insurance, and Documentation Location

Health Conditions

Medications

Guardianship Instructions Documentation Location

Guardian Name

Contact Information

General Instructions of Care – Food, Habits, Exercise, Sleep, and Other Needs

My Dependents – Pets

Name / Type of Pet

Name of Veterinarian

Contact Information

Address

License, Insurance, and Documentation Location

Health Conditions

Medications

Guardianship Instructions Documentation Location

Guardian Name

Contact Information

General Instructions of Care – Food, Habits, Exercise, Sleep, and Other Needs

LOOSE ENDS TO TIE UP

Follow Up: Cancel, Close, Pay, Change of Name, Etc.

Example: Hydro, Electric, Phone, Cable, Internet, Storage, Credit Cards, Autopay, Banking...

Company

Contact Information

Account Number

Username and Password

Notes

Company

Contact Information

Account Number

Username and Password

Notes

Company

Contact Information

Account Number

Username and Password

Notes

Company

Contact Information

Account Number

Username and Password

Notes

Company

Contact Information

Account Number

Username and Password

Notes

Company

Contact Information

Account Number

Username and Password

Notes

Company

Contact Information

Account Number

Username and Password

Notes

Company

Contact Information

Account Number

Username and Password

Notes

Company

Contact Information

Account Number

Username and Password

Notes

Company

Contact Information

Account Number

Username and Password

Notes

Company

Contact Information

Account Number

Username and Password

Notes

Company

Contact Information

Account Number

Username and Password

Notes

Loose Ends to Tie Up Online:

Email, Website, Hosting, Social Media, Banking, Amazon eBay, Memberships

Company

Contact Information

Account Number

Username and Password

Notes

Company

Contact Information

Account Number

Username and Password

Notes

Company

Contact Information

Account Number

Username and Password

Notes

Company

Contact Information

Account Number

Username and Password

Notes

Loose Ends to Tie Up Online:

Company

Contact Information

Account Number

Username and Password

Notes

Company

Contact Information

Account Number

Username and Password

Notes

Company

Contact Information

Account Number

Username and Password

Notes

Company

Contact Information

Account Number

Username and Password

Notes

Loose Ends to Tie Up Online:

Company

Contact Information

Account Number

Username and Password

Notes

Company

Contact Information

Account Number

Username and Password

Notes

Company

Contact Information

Account Number

Username and Password

Notes

Company

Contact Information

Account Number

Username and Password

Notes

MY FINAL WISHES AND INSTRUCTIONS

A MESSAGE TO MY LOVED ONES

Dear

I Am Always With You

Dear

I Am Always With You

Dear

I Am Always With You

Please Remember This

Dear

I Am Always With You

Please Remember This

NOTES

Notes

Notes

Notes

SIGNATURE & DATE

SIGNATURE

Signature

Name and Date